It's me... a Snake

Om KIDZ
An imprint of Om Books International

First Published in 2019 by

Om Kidz | Om Books International

Corporate & Editorial Office
A-12, Sector 64, Noida 201 301
Uttar Pradesh, India
Phone: +91 120 477 4100
Email: editorial@ombooks.com
Website: www.ombooksinternational.com

Sales Office
107, Ansari Road, Darya Ganj
New Delhi 110 002, India
Phone: +91 11 4000 9000
Email: sales@ombooks.com
Website: www.ombooks.com

ISBN: 978-93-86410-52-8

Printed in India

10 9 8 7 6 5 4 3 2 1

Contents

WHO ARE YOU?

Scientific Name

Serpentes

Hello! I am a snake. I belong to the family of reptiles.

Reptiles

Reptiles are a group of animals which have dry, scaly skin.

WHAT ARE YOUR UNIQUE FEATURES?

Most of us are limbless animals. We have a long body and tail. We don't have eyelids.

Pythons and Boa Constrictors

Pythons and Boa Constrictors have tiny hind leg bones near their tail.

Burmese Python

WHERE DO YOU LIVE?

We are found in forests, water, prairies, deserts and on trees. We can adjust to various kinds of habitats.

A new word to learn

Burrow - hole dug by a small animal

Snake Holes

Snakes hide in burrows made by other animals because they cannot make their own **burrows**.

WHY DO YOU SHED YOUR SKIN?

Unlike human skin, our skin doesn't stretch. So, we shed skin as we grow longer. The number of times a snake sheds its skin depends on the age and species of the snake.

Young Snakes

Some young snakes may shed their skin every two weeks.

WHAT DO YOU EAT?

We eat eggs, rats, mice, frogs, toads, cockroaches, lizards and other smaller animals.

Gobble Gobble

We have flexible jaws, which are connected by an elastic **ligament**. The jaws help us eat bigger animals. However, we take a long time to digest our prey.

A new word to learn

Ligament - band of tissues that connect bones and hold organs in place

DO YOU HAVE TEETH?

Yes. We have teeth– 4 rows in the upper jaw and 2 in the lower jaw.

Fangs

Fangs are long, sharp teeth which are connected to the snake's poison sac.

ARE ALL SNAKES POISONOUS?

No, not all snakes are poisonous. Many snakes are harmless and do not have venom or fangs.

Milk Snake

Bull Snake

WHAT DO YOU DO DURING THE DAY?

We spend most of our time resting. We prefer lying in wait for our prey, rather than searching for it.

A new word to learn

Camouflage - the natural colour of an animal makes it look like its surroundings

Camouflage

Snakes use **camouflage** to protect themselves. They can hide under sand or between leaves and trees to escape their enemies.

HOW LONG ARE YOU?

We can be as short as 10 cm or as long as 8.7 m.

Barbados Threadsnakes

Barbados threadsnakes are the smallest species of snakes. These snakes feed on termites and ant larvae.

Reticulated Python

Reticulated pythons are amongst the longest snakes in the world.

DO TWO-HEADED SNAKES ACTUALLY EXIST?

Yes. Two-headed snakes are rare but they can be found both in the wild and in captivity. Two-headed snakes are born when the **embryo** does not divide fully. That's why identical twin snakes don't separate properly.

A new word to learn

Embryo - unborn human or animal in the early stages of growth

CAN SNAKES BE KEPT AS PETS?

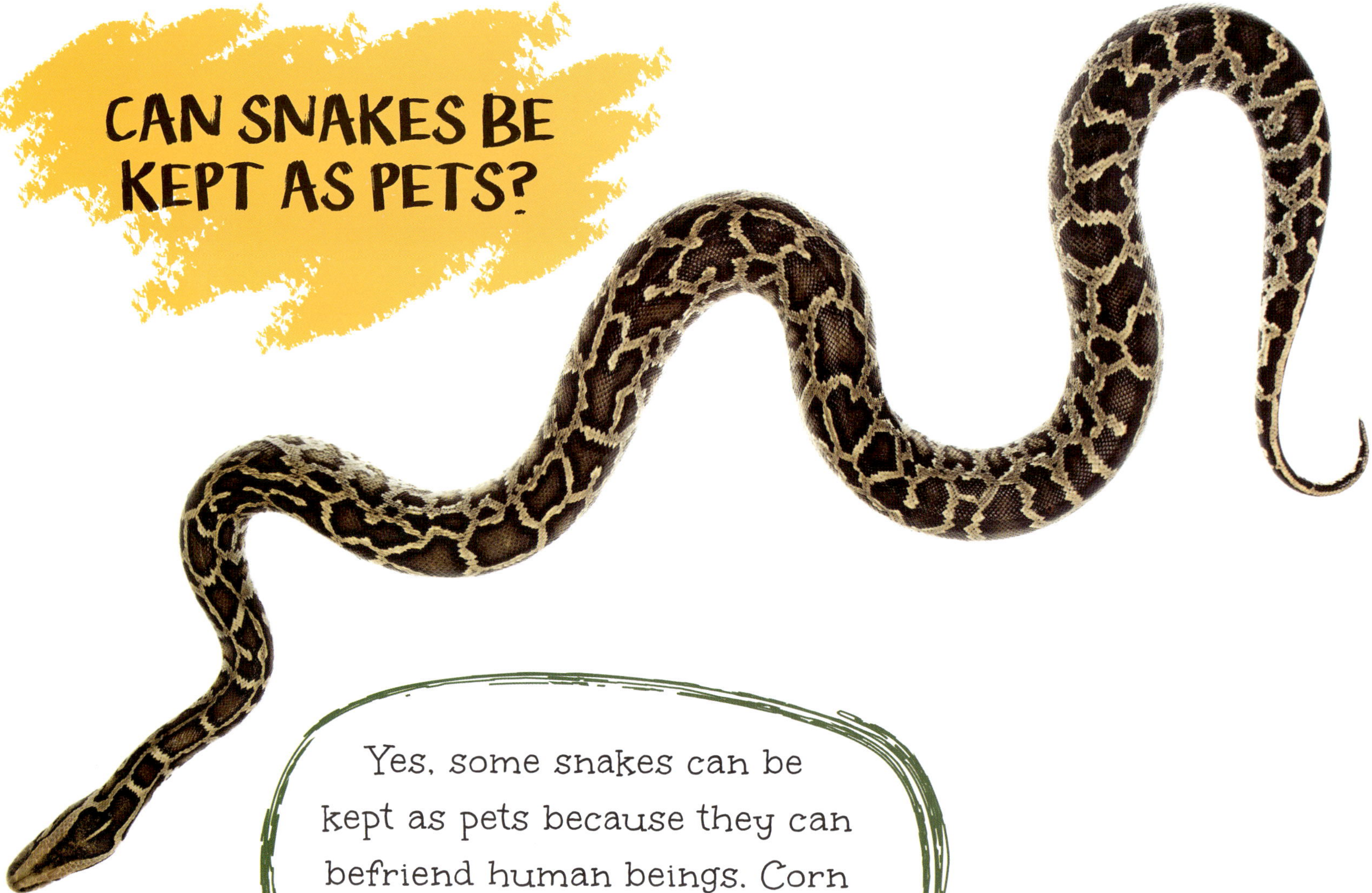

Yes, some snakes can be kept as pets because they can befriend human beings. Corn snakes and Ball pythons are some of the most common pet snakes.

Royal Pythons

Royal Pythons, also known as Ball Pythons, can grow up to 6 ft in length. They have a lifespan of around 30 years.

WHO ARE FLYING SNAKES?

Flying snakes can glide through air for short distances. They make an **undulatory** motion to balance themselves when they **descend**. These snakes are carnivorous and are around 4 ft in length.

A new word to learn

Undulatory - moving in waves

A new word to learn

Descend - move downwards

WHY DO SNAKES FAKE DEATH?

Some snakes such as the Hognose, Grass Snake and Spitting Cobra fake death when they feel threatened. They flip on their back, open their mouth and dangle lifeless to fake death.

Silent Attack

Cobras follow their prey silently, until they are ready to attack.

CAN YOU LIVE WITHOUT FOOD?

Some wild snakes can live without food for long periods, especially during famines. They can go without food for as long as 2 years.

Swallow

Snakes don't chew their food. They swallow their prey whole. Their unique anatomy allows them to digest their prey easily.

CAN YOU CLOSE YOUR EYES?

No, we cannot close our eyes or blink because we have no eyelids. We sleep with our eyes open!

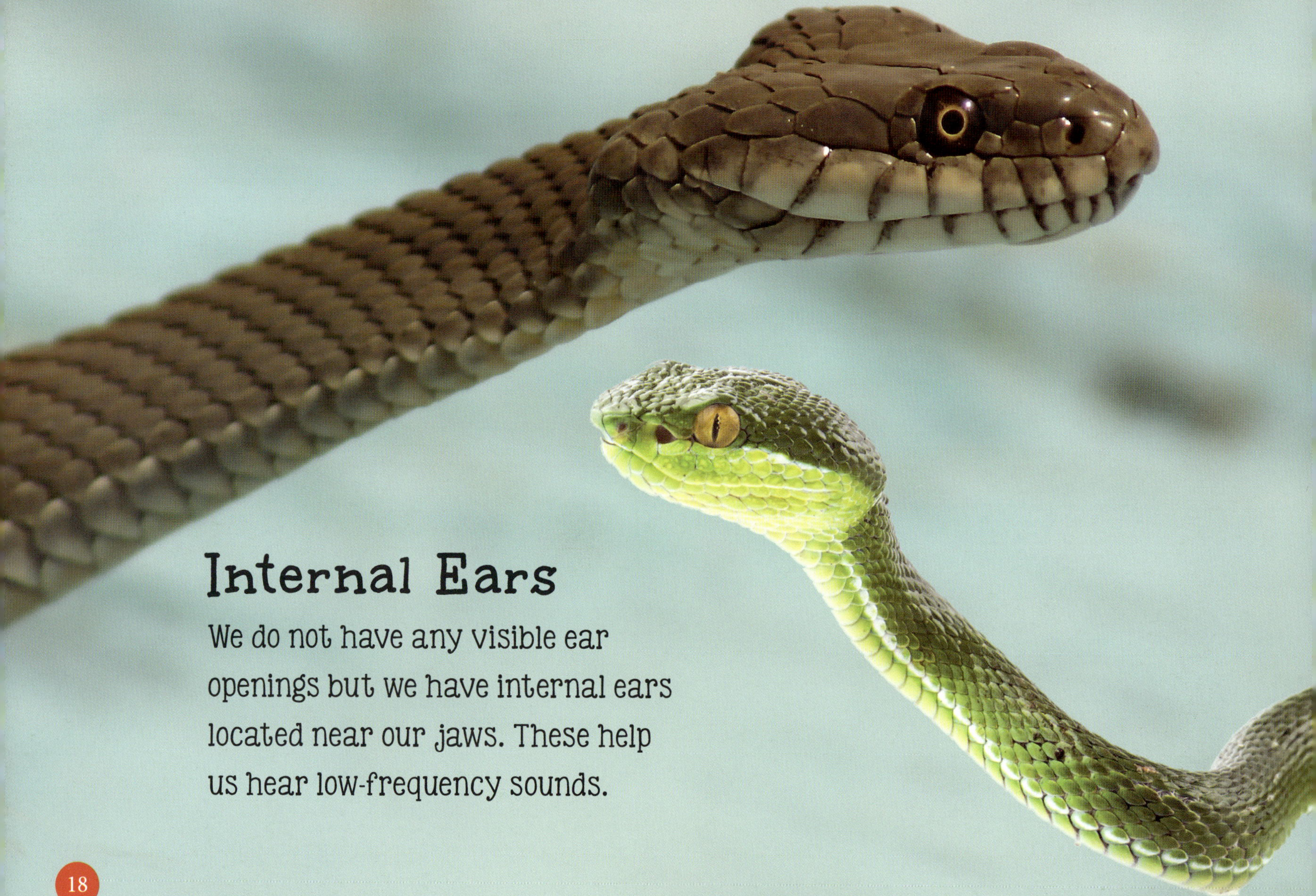

Internal Ears

We do not have any visible ear openings but we have internal ears located near our jaws. These help us hear low-frequency sounds.

DO YOU HAVE A NOSE?

No. We do not have a nose. We use our tongue to smell. We flick our long, forked tongue to pick up particles from the air, ground and water. Our tongue carries these particles to the two small openings on the roof of our mouth.

WHO ARE KING COBRAS?

King cobras are among the longest and most poisonous snakes in the world. They can grow up to 5.6 ft. They are active hunters and they even prey on other snakes.

Hooded Snakes

The hood is one of the most unique features of a cobra. Cobras spread their hoods when they feel threatened.

WHO ARE BLACK MAMBAS?

Incredible Speed

The speed with which Black mambas move helps them to escape their enemies.

Black mambas are the deadliest snakes in the world. They are found in the savannas and the rocky hills of southern and eastern Africa.

Activity Time

Paper Snake

Things You'll Need

- Colourful craft paper
- Scissors
- Glue bottle
- Black marker
- Googly eyes

01 Use blue and yellow craft papers to make the body of the snake. Cut both the sheets of paper into 3-cm strips, lengthwise. Make four strips of each colour.

02 Stick the strips of blue paper to make a long strip. Repeat with the strips of yellow paper.

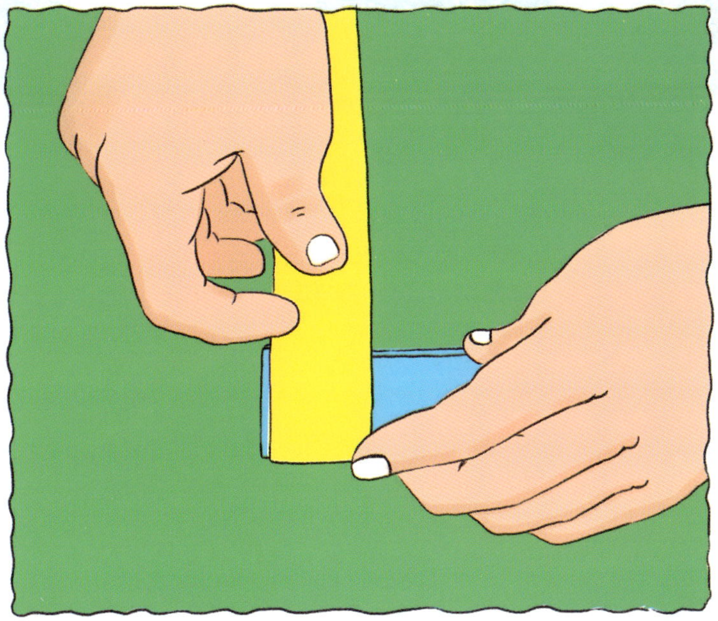

03 Place the blue strip on the table vertically and then place the yellow strip over it horizontally. Line up the strips so that they overlap in a square.

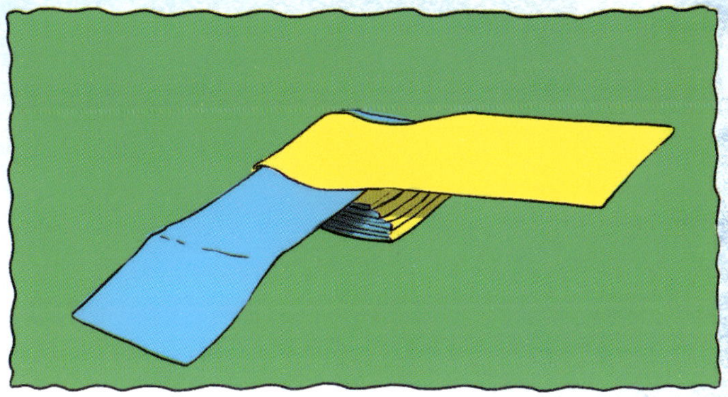

04 Paste the overlapped part together. Then, alternately fold one strip over the other.

05 Fold the strips all the way to the end. Paste the last overlapping section together.

06 Use the yellow craft paper to make the snake's head. Make a forked tongue using blue craft paper. Glue the head to the body of the snake.

07 Paste the googly eyes on the snake's face. Draw the snake's nostrils.

Your paper snake is ready!

The snake is hungry. Help it reach the yummy eggs.